EGYPT

Hello
Bonjour
مرحبا

by Chloe Perkins
illustrated by Tom Woolley

READY-TO-READ

SIMON SPOTLIGHT

An imprint of Simon & Schuster Children's Publishing Division • 1230 Avenue of the Americas, New York, New York 10020 • This Simon Spotlight edition July 2017 • Text copyright © 2017 by Simon & Schuster, Inc. Illustrations copyright © 2017 by Tom Woolley • All rights reserved, including the right of reproduction in whole or in part in any form. SIMON SPOTLIGHT, READY-TO-READ, and colophon are registered trademarks of Simon & Schuster, Inc. For information about special discounts for bulk purchases, please contact Simon & Schuster Special Sales at 1-866-506-1949 or business@simonandschuster.com.
Manufactured in the United States of America 0617 LAK 10 9 8 7 6 5 4 3 2 1
Library of Congress Cataloging-in-Publication Data
Names: Perkins, Chloe, author. | Woolley, Tom, illustrator. Title: Living in . . . Egypt / by Chloe Perkins ; illustrated by Tom Woolley.
Description: New York : Simon Spotlight, an imprint of Simon & Schuster Children's Publishing Division, 2017.
Series: Living in . . . Identifiers: LCCN 2017006179 (print) | LCCN 2017004494 (ebook) | ISBN 9781481497138 (hardcover)
ISBN 9781481497121 (trade pbk.) | ISBN 9781481497145 (ebook) Subjects: LCSH: Egypt—Social life and customs—Juvenile literature.
Classification: LCC DT70 .P47 2017 (ebook) | LCC DT70 (print) | DDC 962—dc23 LC record available at https://lccn.loc.gov/2017006179

GLOSSARY

BCE/CE: how years are measured on the Western calendar; BCE stands for "Before the Common Era," and the year increases as it is further back in time; CE stands for "Common Era," and the year increases as it is further forward in time

Crop: a plant or something that comes from a plant, such as fruits or vegetables

Mecca: the holy city in Islam; one of the pillars of Islam is taking a pilgrimage, or holy journey, to this city

Monument: a statue, building, or structure built to honor something or someone

Pyramid: a large structure built with a square base and four sides that come together to form a point at the top

Ramadan: the ninth month of the Muslim calendar, during which Muslims celebrate when the Prophet Muhammad (peace be upon him) first heard the word of God

Region: a place with certain geographic features that make it different from the surrounding area

Sphinx: a creature from mythology that had the body of a lion, a human head, and sometimes wings

Temple: a building used to practice one's religion

Trade: the act of selling, buying, or otherwise swapping goods

NOTE TO READERS: Some of these words may have more than one definition. The definitions above are how these words are used in this book.

Ahlan wa Sahlan!
(say: AH-lahn wah sah-LAHN)
That means "hi" in Arabic.
My name is Amira, and I
live in Egypt. Egypt is a country
in Africa where more than ninety
million people live . . .
including me!

Egypt is in the northeast
corner of Africa. It is part
of a region called the
Middle East.
Much of the Middle East
is hot and dry. It is
covered with deserts.

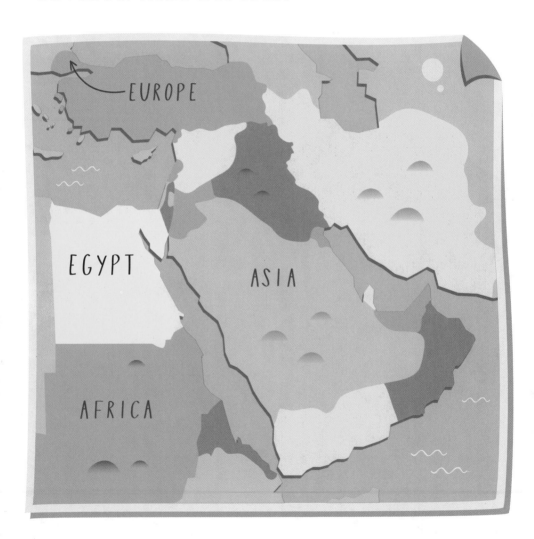

Almost all of Egypt's land is desert. The two largest deserts in Egypt are the Eastern Desert and the Western Desert. Animals such as cobras, hyenas (say: hi-EE-nahs), lynxes (say: LINKS-es), and gazelles can be found there.

The rest of Egypt's land is along the Nile River.
The Nile River is the longest river in the world. It starts south of Egypt, at the equator. It cuts through eastern Egypt, flowing from the south to the north, where it empties into the Mediterranean Sea.

In the north, near the
Mediterranean Sea,
is the Nile River Delta.
The land in the delta is
perfect for growing crops,
so this area is covered in farms.
The south of Egypt has lots of
mountains and hills.

Along the Nile are many big cities, like Cairo (say: KY-roh). Cairo is our capital and the largest city in Egypt. Near Cairo is Giza (say: GEE-zuh). At Giza are some of the coolest ancient monuments in Egypt, like the pyramids and the Great Sphinx (say: sfinks).

Alexandria is on the Mediterranean Sea. It was founded by the ancient king Alexander the Great.

Port Said (say: sy-EED) is where many goods come into Egypt through the Suez Canal. The canal connects the Mediterranean and Red Seas and is important for trade.

I live in an apartment in Cairo with my dad, grandma, and older sister.

My dad owns a coffee shop down the street.

There are lots of coffee shops in Cairo, but his is the best!

My dad is often busy at work, so my grandma helps take care of my sister and me.

My sister loves fashion. She wants to design clothes when she grows up.

Each morning my grandma, sister, and I eat breakfast together. My dad has to get up extra early to open the shop, so he's already at work. Once my sister and I are ready, my grandma drives us to school.

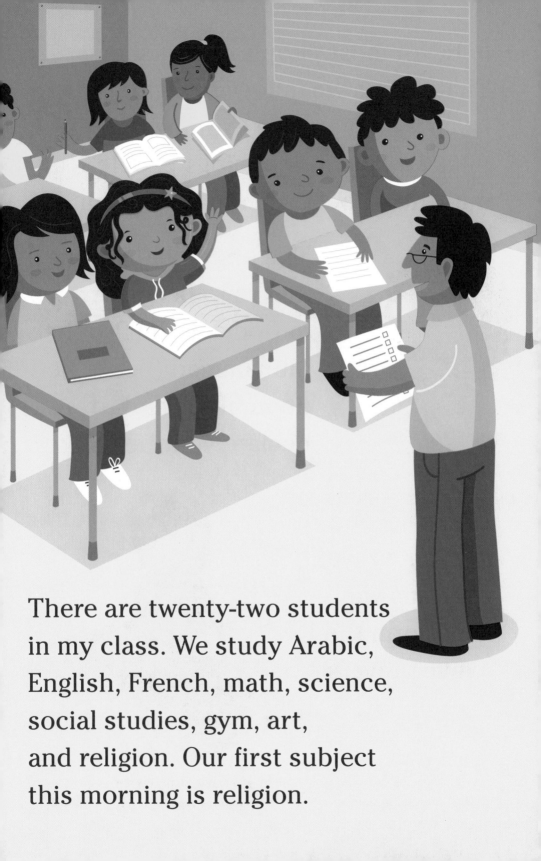

There are twenty-two students
in my class. We study Arabic,
English, French, math, science,
social studies, gym, art,
and religion. Our first subject
this morning is religion.

In Egypt most people are Muslim. That means we follow a religion called Islam. Today we are learning the five pillars of Islam, the things people must do or believe in to be Muslim.

The first pillar, faith, means to believe in God and the Prophet Muhammad (peace be upon him)* and to declare your belief.

The second pillar, prayer, means we perform the five prayers each day.

*Muslims always say "peace be upon him" when we talk about a prophet or angel. A prophet is someone who delivers messages from God to people.

The third pillar, charity, means helping those in need.

The fourth pillar, fasting, means we don't eat or drink during daytime in the month of Ramadan.

Pilgrimage, the fifth pillar, means visiting Mecca if you're able.

After religion we study languages.
I speak English, Arabic, and French!
English and French are hard to
write. The languages are different,
but they both use the same alphabet
and are written left to right.
Arabic has its own alphabet
and is written right to left.

Snack time! My grandma
packed me chips and a sandwich.
Yum! After we finish our snacks,
we have gym class. Then we move on
to our social studies lesson. History is
my favorite subject.
Egypt has a really long history!

Around 5000 BCE people began living along the Nile River. Around 3100 BCE, these people invented one of the oldest written languages in the world, called hieroglyphics (say: hi-roh-GLIF-iks). Some hieroglyphics looked a lot like pictures, and more than seven hundred symbols were used.

Hieroglyphics could be read forward, backward, or even down!
To know which way the words should be read, you looked at which way the symbols were facing. Ancient Egyptians used hieroglyphics to write poetry, keep records, and tell stories about their gods and rulers.

For many centuries Egypt was split into the upper and lower kingdoms. But around 3100 BCE a king united the kingdoms. Over the next two thousand years Egypt blossomed. Ancient Egyptians invented things we use today, like toothbrushes, locks, and eye makeup!

Egyptians built monuments for their
rulers, or pharaohs (say: FAIR-ohs).
Many of them still stand today, like
the Great Sphinx, the Karnak Temple,
and more than one hundred pyramids.
Egypt also became a center for trade.
People from all over the world
came here to buy and sell things.

But two thousand years later Egypt was weakening. The kingdom was overthrown many times, including by Alexander the Great of Greece in 332 BCE. After being part of many empires, Egypt was taken over by Arab Muslims from modern day Saudi Arabia in 642 CE.

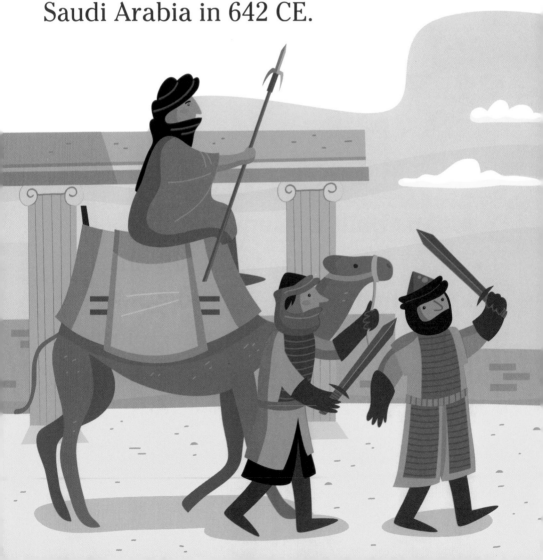

When Arab Muslims took over Egypt, they brought their religion, language, and culture too. Over hundreds of years, many people chose to follow Islam and learn the Arabic language.

That's all we've learned so far!
After history we study math, art,
and science, and then school is over.
My grandma picks up my sister and me
from school at three o'clock.
My dad takes a break from work,
and we eat a big lunch together.

Today we are eating
kushari (say: KOO-shah-ree).
Kushari is a dish of pasta, rice,
lentils, chickpeas, and onions,
topped with tomato sauce.
I like mine extra spicy with
hot sauce, too! As we eat,
we talk about
the upcoming
holiday.

Ramadan is the ninth month in the Muslim calendar, and it starts next week! Remember the five pillars of Islam? During Ramadan we fast, which means we don't eat or drink from sunrise to sunset. We have a big meal before sunrise and then another big meal at night with friends.

Kids like me don't have to fast, but I want to try it. Last year I fasted for one morning, but this year I'm going to fast for one whole day! As part of Ramadan we also pray more and give money to charities or volunteer. At the end of Ramadan we have a big celebration.

After lunch I watch TV, and then I do my homework. This afternoon I'm helping my sister make a new hijab (say: hee-JOB). A hijab is a head covering that Muslim women wear in public or when they pray. I'll wear a hijab when I'm older too. I hope my sister will make me a cool hijab like this!

It's dinnertime! In Egypt
dinner is a small meal.
We often eat our leftovers
from lunch or have
something light like
molokheyyah (say: moh-loh-KAY-yah).
Molokheyyah is a vegetable soup
made with garlic and other spices.

After dinner it's time for the
evening prayers. I'm not old
enough to do the five prayers most
Muslims do each day, but I do know
how to pray *Isha* (say: EE-shah),
the nightly prayer. When I pray,
I wear a hijab like my grandma
and sister, and stand on a prayer rug.

After prayers it's time for bed.
My sister and I flip through her
fashion magazines before we go
to sleep. We see pictures of fashion
shows in Italy and Japan and India!
I would like to go to all of
these places. Would you like to
visit Egypt someday?

ALL ABOUT
EGYPT!

NAME: Arab Republic of Egypt (or Egypt for short!)

POPULATION: 95 million

CAPITAL: Cairo

LANGUAGE: Arabic is the official language of Egypt, but many people also speak English and French, just like Amira!

TOTAL AREA: 386,662 square miles

GOVERNMENT: presidential republic

CURRENCY: Egyptian pound

FUN FACT: In ancient times the city of Alexandria was said to have the largest library in the world. The library was destroyed long ago, but today a new library stands in its place. In addition to books, this new library has preserved copies of billions of websites going back to 1996.

FLAG: Equal-sized horizontal bands of red (representing struggle) and black (representing the end of oppression) with a third band of white (representing peace and freedom) between them. In the center of the flag is the national emblem.